P·A·S·S·O·V·E·R
SEDER

Ritual and Menu for an Observance by Christians

by Barbara Balzac Thompson

Augsburg Publishing House

Minneapolis

CONTENTS

PASSOVER SEDER
Ritual and Menu for an Observance by Christians

International Standard Book No. 0-8066-2133-8

Copyright © 1984 Augsburg Publishing House

Cover art by Judy Swanson.
Illustrations by RKB Studios.

MANUFACTURED IN THE UNITED STATES OF AMERICA

INTRODUCTION

In compiling this book to help Christians experience the meaning of the Jewish Seder, I drew heavily on my personal experience of growing up in Los Angeles in a Conservative Jewish home. The Seder is presented as I recall watching my paternal grandfather lead us through the ritual meal and hearing him tell the stories of times past.

As one who was baptized into Christ in 1974 I want to emphasize that the Seder is not a Christian observance. It belongs to the Jewish tradition. In that form it is a historical, vivid, and beautiful expression of God's action for his people.

The Seder is one part of the present-day Jewish seven-day Passover celebration. The name Passover harks back to the time when God, through Moses, led the Israelites out of their slavery. The Egyptian pharaoh was finally convinced to let the people go when the angel of death killed every firstborn in Egypt but "passed over" the Israelite homes that had put lamb's blood on their doorposts.

To recall that great deliverance, the elements of the traditional Seder meal symbolize historically significant features of the Israelite experience. Both the event of God's deliverance and the directions God gave Moses for later commemoration of the Passover history are represented in the Seder ritual and meal.

Christians are particularly interested in this ritual meal because it was during a Passover celebration that Jesus instituted Holy Communion. It should be realized, however, that the Passover clearly predates and is entirely separate from the Eucharist. The Seder is a later Jewish form of the Passover observance, useful and important in its own right, having been practiced for more than 1,000 years. It must not be mixed with Christian concepts or expressions if it is to be authentic. It is a Jewish celebration of freedom useful in helping Christians understand Judaism.

Christians will want to avoid any tendency to syncretism, that is, mixing the Seder and the Lord's Supper so that the Seder appears to be a Christian observance. It is a Jewish ritual used to observe the Passover. The Lord's Supper is a Christian sacrament which was instituted by our Lord following a specific Passover observance.

Apart from its observance in the synagogue, Pesach (páy-sak), which is the Passover, has a unique place in the Jewish home because of the Seder and because of the changed atmosphere in the home during the seven days of celebration. The atmosphere in the home is created each year by specific traditional practices. The home is carefully cleaned and scrubbed in all its parts, cooking vessels are made kosher, and all chametz (leavened bread, some foods, and ordinary dishes and cooking vessels) are removed or koshered (where possible) for the welcome of Pesach. Some foods are completely forbidden for use during Passover. Other foods must carry the "Kosher for Passover" label with rabbinical signature.

BEDIKAT CHAMETZ

It is customary to search for leaven (chametz) on the evening preceding the first Seder. The ceremony consists of placing a small crumb of bread in each

3

room of the house (excepting the washrooms) and "searching" for it by the light of a candle. When a crumb is "found" it is brushed into a wooden (or plastic) spoon with a feather (or a toothbrush). All of the leaven, together with the implements used in the search, are tied together in a cloth and disposed of by burning the following morning prior to 10 A.M. This ceremony is symbolic of the removal of every last crumb of leaven from Jewish homes before Passover so that no leaven can be seen or found in the home. Prior to beginning the search for leaven, the following blessing (brachah) is said:

Praised be you, O Lord our God, King of the universe, who has sanctified us with your commandments and enjoined upon us the joy (mitzvah) of removing leaven before the Passover (Pesach).

After the search is completed, the following legal declaration is made:

May all leaven in my possession which I have not seen or removed be regarded as mere dust of the earth.

It is forbidden by Jewish law to possess any chametz for Passover. The Torah declares: "It (leaven) shall not be seen, and it shall not be found for seven days." All leaven or food not specifically permitted for Passover use must be disposed of prior to 10 A.M. preceding the first Seder. Actually all chametz should be physically removed from Jewish homes for the entire Passover holiday. Chametz which remains in the ownership of a Jew during Passover is forbidden to be used after Passover. Jews are enjoined by the sages of Israel to legally (as well as physically) dispossess themselves of all chametz. This is done by arranging for the legal "sale," to a non-Jew, of all the chametz in their possession.

The rabbi customarily acts as agent for this legal transfer of ownership. By means of a document (shtar mehirah), the congregant authorizes the rabbi to "sell" all of the chametz in his or her possession:

I _____
(name)   (address)

hereby authorize Rabbi _____ to sell *all* of my chametz wherever it may be found before Passover.

_____
(signature)

It is customary to refrain from eating regular matzah prior to the Seder, but egg matzah may be eaten from 10 A.M. of the morning of the first Seder until the Seder.

THE SEDER TABLE

The Seder meal and ritual properly occur on the first evening of Passover. *(The Jewish day begins with evening.)*
The Seder table may be one table for a small group or a family or a number of tables for a larger gathering. The finest dinnerware and tableware available for the size of the group and the resources of the gathering should be used; also use a good tablecloth.

Included on each table should be a low floral centerpiece or flowers laid long-stemmed down the center of the table, as well as lighted candles. The centerpiece and candlesticks on the leader's table should be especially attractive.

4

A fine Seder plate *(which can be purchased)* or ornate platter should be in front of the leader conducting the Seder. On this plate are the following:

1. A roasted shankbone of a lamb *(not to be eaten)*
2. A roasted egg *(puncture one end of egg and roast at 300-350° till shell turns brown; not to be eaten)*
3. Bitter herbs *(often coarsely ground horseradish)*
4. Charoset, a mixture of chopped, peeled apples, coarsely chopped walnuts, cinnamon, mixed with Concord grape wine, to taste
5. Parsley, lettuce, or watercress, cut into small pieces

In addition there should be near the leader:

Three matzot, placed in a specially designed matzah cover or in the folds of a large cloth dinner napkin.

There should also be on all tables:

Very salty water in small bowls within reach of everyone.

A wine goblet at each place, plus a large goblet, filled with wine, at the center of the table. The large goblet is the cup of Elijah.

Extra dishes of bitter herbs and charoset will be necessary for large gatherings.

A pillow should be on the left arm of the leader's chair or available nearby. Each person at the Seder should have a pillow or cushion for ''reclining.''

A box of matzah and a bottle of wine, labeled Kosher for Passover, should be supplied for every 8-10 people present. Also needed for each unit that size are a pitcher of water, a bowl of hot water, and a large linen towel *(to wash and dry hands),* and a haggadah or service book.

NOTE: During the Seder the middle matzah will be broken in two. One half will be placed back in the cloth and the other set aside for dessert (afikomen). The dessert is customarily ''stolen'' by one of the children, and in order for the Seder to continue, the dessert must be ransomed.

THE SEDER HAGGADAH

Biblical References

Exodus 12—13	2 Chronicles 30
Deuteronomy 7:6-9	2 Chronicles 35:1-19
Deuteronomy 16	Joshua 5:10-12

L = Leader

A = Assembled People

(The family is seated around the table.)

הַגָּדָה

L   We are about to recite the ancient story of Israel's redemption from bondage in Egypt. The purpose of this Seder is to afford us the opportunity to recall the dramatic and miraculous events which led to the exodus from an ancient land of slavery. The Old Testament, centuries ago, instructed us to meet, as we do tonight, when it declared, "And you shall tell your son on that day, saying: It is because of what the Lord did for me when I came out of Egypt" (Exod. 13:8). Exodus 12:14, 43 and 13:8-10 instruct the Jewish people that young and old should gather on the eve of Passover in order that older people might relate to the children, and to all, this thrilling chapter in the history of our people (Lev. 23:5-7; Num. 9:5).

L   We have before us three MATZOT commemorating the bread which our forefathers were compelled to eat during their hasty departure from Egypt (Exod. 12:15, 17-20; Lev. 23:6). We use three matzot to represent the three religious groupings of the Jewish people—Kohen, Levi, and Yisroayl. They are placed together to indicate the unity of the Jewish people. In unity Jewish people find their strength and power to survive.

L   The second symbol is the ROASTED SHANKBONE which reminds us of the Paschal lamb, a special animal sacrifice which our ancestors offered on the altar of the great temple in Jerusalem on the Passover holiday (Exod. 12:3-13).

L   The third symbol is a ROASTED EGG which reminds us of a second offering brought to the temple on Passover. It was known as the festival offering, for it was brought on each of the three festivals—Pesach, Shavuot, and Succot.

L   The fourth symbol is the MOROR, the bitter herb, which reminds us of the bitterness of slavery, which our ancestors were compelled to endure (Exod. 12:8).

L   The fifth symbol is the CHAROSET, a mixture of apples, walnuts, wine, and cinnamon, made to resemble the mortar with which our ancestors made bricks for the building of Egyptian cities (Exod. 1:8-14, 3:7-9, 5:7-9).

L   The final symbol is the KARPAS, a green vegetable, used to remind us that Pesach coincides with the arrival of spring and the gathering of the spring harvest. Passover, in ancient times, was also an agricultural festival and an occasion on which our ancestors gave thanks for the earth's rich bounties.

L Four times, in the course of this service, we shall partake of the wine, symbol of joy and thanksgiving. The four cups represent the four-fold promise which God made to the Israelites in Egypt. In the following words, he assured them that they would be freed from servitude:

"I will bring you out . . . and I will deliver you . . . and I will redeem you . . . and I will take you" (Exod. 6:6-7).

L These are the symbols of Passover—echoes of the past and reminders of the present. As we partake of them, may we remember the events which they recall and may we embody their spirit in our present-day endeavors. We shall now sanctify the holiday with the recitation of the Kadaysh.

KADAYSH

קַדֵּשׁ

(At a large gathering one woman from each table now lights the candles and one man fills the wine glasses. In a home celebration the woman of the house and the man of the house do these tasks.)

L Please stand.

A Blessed are you, O Lord our God, King of the universe, who created the fruit of the vine. Blessed are you, O Lord our God, who has chosen us for your service from among the nations, exalting us by making us holy through your commandments (Deut. 7:6). In love have you given us, O Lord our God, holidays for joy and festivals for gladness. You did give us this Feast of Unleavened Bread, the season of freedom, in commemoration of our liberation from Egypt. You have chosen us for your service from among the nations and have sanctified us by giving us, with love and gladness, your holy festivals as a heritage. Blessed are you, O Lord, who hallowed Israel and the festivals.

A Blessed are you, O Lord our God, King of the universe, who has kept us in life, who has preserved us and has enabled us to reach this season.

(Drink first cup of wine.)

L Please be seated.

URCHATZ

וּרְחַץ

L The second ceremony of the Seder is known as Urchatz, Washing of the Hands. This is a symbolic act of purification, which precedes our participation in this religious service.

KARPAS

כַּרְפַּס

L The third ceremony is partaking of the Karpas. We now dip this green fruit of the earth into salt water, as we recite together:

A In partaking of this fruit of the earth, we give thanks to God for all his bounties. We also recall that our ancestors were tillers of the soil and were ever grateful for the earth's produce. In tasting of the salt water, we are asked to remember the tears which they shed while suffering the tortures of slavery. May our gratitude for the blessings which we enjoy help to soften the pain of sorrow, and convert tears to joy and appreciation.

A Blessed are you, O Lord our God, King of the universe, who created the fruit of the earth.

(The karpas is eaten.)

YACHATZ

L We now perform the ceremony of Yachatz. I shall break the middle matzah in two, removing one half and setting it aside. This will become the Afikomen, the dessert, to be eaten at the conclusion of our meal.

(Afikomen is the Greek term. The leader breaks middle matzah, wraps half in a napkin, and places it in any convenient place.)

יַחַץ

MAGEED

L *(Raises up the three matzot and says:)* Lo! This is the bread of affliction, the humble and simple bread which our ancestors ate in the land of Egypt. Let those who are hungry join us at this Seder, and let them partake of what we have to share.

A With gratitude for the blessings which we have been given, we invite the less fortunate to share with us at this meal and also at other times.

L May the Jewish people, wherever they are, those still deprived of total freedom, enjoy that liberty at this time next year.

A May our people in Israel speedily attain freedom from fear and want and be privileged to build a symbol of peace for all the nations.

(Wine glasses are refilled.)

מַגִּיד

THE FOUR QUESTIONS

(Note of interest: Traditionally the youngest child able to chant in Hebrew will recite all four questions here. For this observance, however, the four questions may be assigned to four young children.)

Child 1 Why is this night different from all other nights?
On all other nights we eat either chametz (leavened bread) or matzah, but on this night we eat only matzah.

Child 2 On all other nights we eat all kinds of herbs, but on this night we eat only moror.

Child 3 On all other nights we do not dip even once, but on this night we dip twice.

Child 4 On all other nights we eat either sitting or reclining, but on this night we eat reclining.

Answers to the Children's Questions

A   Once we were slaves to Pharaoh in Egypt, and the Lord, in his goodness and mercy, brought us forth from that land with a mighty hand and an outstretched arm.

L   Had he not rescued us from the hand of Pharaoh, surely we and our children would still be enslaved, deprived of liberty and human dignity.

A   We, therefore, gather year after year to retell this ancient story. For, in reality, it is not ancient but eternal in its message and its spirit.

L   The first question asked concerns the use of matzah. We eat these unleavened cakes to remember that our ancestors, in their haste to leave Egypt, could not wait for bread to rise, and so removed them from the ovens while still flat (Exod. 12:34).

A   To the second question we reply: We partake of the moror on this night that we might taste of some bitterness, to remind ourselves how bitter is the lot of one caught in the grip of slavery (Exod. 12:8).

L   Thirdly, we dip twice in the course of this service, greens in salt water and moror in charoset; once to replace tears with gratefulness, and once to sweeten bitterness and suffering.

A   The fourth question asks why, on this night, we eat in a reclining position. To recline at mealtimes in ancient days was a sign of freedom. On this night of Passover we demonstrate our sense of complete freedom by reclining during our repast.

THE LORD'S PROMISE

L   Blessed is God who fulfills his promises, who is ever faithful to his servants who trust in him.

A   The Lord foretold the events of Israel's bondage when relating to Abraham the future of his children.

L   Then God described the years of their service on foreign soil, tormented by a strange and hostile people (Gen. 15:13).

A   It was then that God also promised to rescue and redeem them, bringing judgment upon the cruel oppressor (Gen. 15:14-16).

L   Great has been the Lord's divine promise, fulfilled and realized in days past.

A   Great have been God's promises in all ages, source of hope to a stricken and downtrodden people.

(All raise their cups.)

L   In every age oppressors rose against us, to crush our spirit and bring us low.

A   From the hands of all these tyrants and conquerors, the Lord rescued and restored his people.

L   Not in Egypt alone did Israel face the threat of total annihilation.

A   In many lands and many ages, the flame of Jewish life faced the fierce winds of tyranny.

9

L   In all these battles and desperate struggles, God's help and guidance assured our survival.

A   Our hope is strong and our faith unshakable, that no enemy shall ever triumph over Israel.

(Cups are put down.)

THE STORY OF ISRAEL IN THE LAND OF EGYPT

Participant   Scripture tells that in the land of Canaan, at the time of a famine, our patriarch, Jacob, sent his sons to Egypt to purchase food. They sought permission from Pharaoh to allow their flocks to graze, for the pasture lands in Canaan were barren. It was not their intention to settle in Egypt; merely to find relief from want (Gen. 42:1-3).

Participant   There were but 70 people who arrived in Egypt, but, in time, their number increased. Soon they grew in strength and became a mighty people. The Egyptians came to fear them for, they reasoned, in time of war they might join with enemy nations and become a threatening force. They, therefore, decided to subdue them with forced labor and to reduce their numbers by casting male children into the river. Taskmasters were placed over the Hebrews. The taskmasters whipped and tortured them, compelling them to make bricks and build great cities for Pharaoh (Gen. 46:27b, 47:27, Exod. 1:7-14).

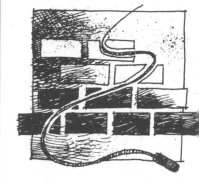

Participant   The task was inhuman and too great to bear. The Jewish people cried out to God and he heard their cry. He called to Moses, charging him to appear before Pharaoh and to demand that the people be released. Pharaoh was obstinate and would not heed the word of God. It was then that Moses foretold the punishment which the Almighty would bring upon Pharaoh and the Egyptians: plagues would be visited upon the land of Egypt in which many would perish. In the face of all pleas, Pharaoh refused to free the Jewish people. In consequence, the plagues descended upon Egypt. Many perished and the suffering was great. Pharaoh, nonetheless, remained obstinate; he would not yield. When the tenth plague was visited upon them, the death of the firstborn, a great cry went up throughout Egypt, and Pharaoh finally ordered Moses to take his people out of the land (Exod. 2:9-10, 23-25; 7:17–12:29).

TEN PLAGUES

L   When people defy the will of God, they bring pain and suffering upon themselves. God's Law aims for the welfare and happiness of all humankind. To deny his Law and to do evil brings destruction upon those who perpetrate it.

A   When Pharaoh defied the command of God to release the Jewish people, he invited adversity upon himself and his own people.

L Though the plagues that were visited upon the Egyptians were the result of their own evil, we do not rejoice over their downfall and defeat. Judaism regards all people as children of God, even enemies who seek to destroy our people.

A When, for the sake of our welfare, they meet with suffering and death, we mourn their loss and express sorrow over their destruction.

L A full cup is the symbol of complete joy. Though we celebrate the triumph of our sacred cause, our happiness is not complete so long as others have to be sacrificed for its sake. Therefore, we shall diminish the wine in our cups as we recall the plagues visited upon the Egyptians, to give expression to our sorrow over the losses which each plague exacted. We now recite the list of Ten Plagues, pouring off wine as each one is mentioned.

(Dip finger into wine and put drop onto plate as each plague is mentioned.)

Blood	Beasts	Locusts
Frogs	Boils	Darkness
Gnats	Hail	Slaying of
Flies		firstborn

DAYENU

דַּיֵּנוּ

L Great and numerous are the kindnesses which the Lord extended to our fathers, for each of them we offer thanks and humble gratitude.

A Any one of these would have been sufficient to show his love for us, his pity and compassion.

L With great loving-kindness he redeemed us from Egypt, executing judgment upon our oppressors and the idols they worshiped.

A With awesome might he divided the Red Sea, allowing our people safe passage (Exod. 14:13-29).

L With tender care he protected us in the wilderness, granting shelter from the ravages of desert life.

A For 40 years he provided for all our needs, sending manna from heaven, food and water to sustain us (Exod. 16:4-16).

L With abundant love he gave us the Sabbath, to afford rest and refreshment for body and soul (Exod. 16:22-30).

A To Mount Sinai he brought us at an hour supreme and gave us the Torah, the crown of our life (Exod. 19:1–23:19; 24:12; 20:1-17—Ten Commandments).

L In triumphant spirit he led us into the land of Israel where inspired leaders did build the Holy Temple.

A How great and numerous are the kindnesses which the Lord has shown us; for each act of goodness we are abundantly grateful!

(Sing DAYENU. See music on page 12.)

Dayenu

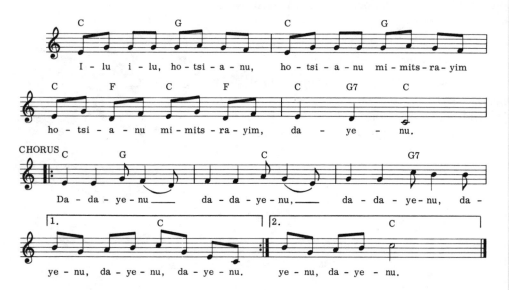

I - lu i - lu, ho - tsi - a - nu, ho - tsi - a - nu mi - mits - ra - yim

ho - tsi - a - nu mi - mits - ra - yim, da - ye - nu.

CHORUS

Da - da - ye - nu ___ da - da - ye - nu, ___ da - da - ye - nu, da -

1. ye - nu, da - ye - nu, da - ye - nu.

2. ye - nu, da - ye - nu.

Additional Verses

2 I-lu i-lu na-tan la-nu na-tan la-nu et ha-Sha-bat, da-ye-nu.

3 I-lu i-lu na-tan la-nu na-tan la-nu et ha-Torah, da-ye-nu.

4 I-lu i-lu hih-ni-sa-nu hih-ni-sa-nu l'E-rets Yis-ra-el, da-ye-nu.

Translation

1 Had he done nothing more than take us out of Egypt, dayenu (for that alone we should have been grateful).

2 Had he given us the Sabbath and nothing more, dayenu.

3 Had he given us the Torah and nothing more, dayenu.

4 Had he brought us into the land of Israel, dayenu.

THE THREE SYMBOLS

Biblical Reference

Exodus 12

Rabbi Gamaliel said: "Whoever has not explained the three symbols of Passover has not fulfilled his responsibilities." The responsibilities are to give the following instructions:

Participant: *(Pointing to roasted shankbone on Seder plate)* What is the significance of the Pesach, the Paschal lamb, symbolized by this shankbone, which our ancestors ate in the days when the temple was in existence? It served as a reminder that the Lord "posach"— passed over—the homes of the Jews when he smote the firstborn of the Egyptians.

Participant: *(Holding up cake of matzah)* What is the significance of the matzah? It is the flat, unleavened bread that our people ate during their departure from Egypt, for in their haste they could not wait for the dough to rise.

Participant: *(Pointing to the bitter herbs)* What is the significance of these bitter herbs? They serve to remind us that the Egyptians embittered the lives of our ancestors, as the Torah relates: "So they made the people of Israel serve with rigor, and made their lives bitter with hard service, in mortar and brick, and in all kinds of work in the field; in all their work they made them serve with rigor" (Exod. 1:13-14).

OUR PERSONAL DELIVERANCE
B'CHOL

In every generation, each Jew must look upon himself or herself as though he or she, personally, was among those who went forth from Egypt. Not our ancestors alone did the Holy One, blessed be he, redeem from suffering, but also us and our families.

L The struggle for freedom is a continuous struggle, for never do human beings reach total liberty and opportunity.

A In every age, some new freedom is won and established, adding to the advancement of human happiness and security.

L Yet, each age uncovers a formerly unrecognized servitude, requiring new liberation to set human souls free.

A In every age, the concept of freedom grows broader, widening the horizons for finer and nobler living.

L Each generation is duty-bound to contribute to this growth, else humankind's ideals become stagnant and stationary.

A The events in Egypt were but the beginning of a force in history which will forever continue.

L In this spirit we see ourselves as participants in the Exodus, for we must dedicate our energies to the cause there begun.

בְּכָל

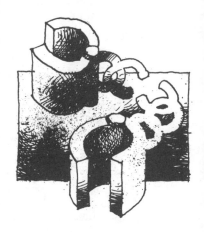

A In our day we shall defend the heritage of liberty taught by the Torah and preserved by God's goodness through human forms of government. *(All raise their cups.)* As inheritors of the priceless heritage of liberty, we join now in praising and glorifying God's holy name. For the miracles which he wrought in the past and also in our day, we offer him our thankfulness. He delivered us from slavery to freedom, from sorrow to happiness, from mourning to rejoicing, from darkness to light. In gratitude for these manifold blessings, we shall sing songs of praise to him.

(The cups are put down and refilled.)

HALLEL

הַלֵּל

(Read responsively.)

Psalm 113

Hallelujah!

Give praise, you servants of the Lord;
  praise the name of the Lord.

Let the name of the Lord be blessed,
  from this time forth forevermore.

From the rising of the sun
  to its going down
  let the name of the Lord be praised.

The Lord is high above all nations,
  and his glory above the heavens.

Who is like the Lord our God,
  who sits enthroned on high,
  but stoops to behold
  the heavens and the earth?

He takes up the weak out of the dust
  and lifts up the poor from the ashes.

He sets them with the princes,
  with the princes of his people.

He makes the woman
  of a childless house
  to be a joyful mother of children.

Praise the Lord!

Psalm 114

Hallelujah!

When Israel came out of Egypt,
  the house of Jacob
  from a people of strange speech,

Judah became God's sanctuary
  and Israel his dominion.

The sea beheld it and fled;
  Jordan turned and went back.

The mountains skipped like rams,
  and the little hills like young sheep.

What ailed you, O sea, that you fled,
  O Jordan, that you turned back,

you mountains,
that you skipped like rams,
  you little hills like young sheep?

Tremble, O earth,
at the presence of the Lord,
  at the presence of the God of Jacob,

who turned the hard rock
into a pool of water
  and flint-stone into a flowing spring.

(After reading, cups are raised and the following is recited.)

A Blessed are you, O Lord our God, King of the universe, who has redeemed us and our ancestors from Egypt and has brought us to this occasion to partake of the matzah and the moror.

L May it be your will, our God and God of our forebears, to grant us life and to bring us, in peace, to many more festivals, holy days, and happy celebrations.

A May those occasions inspire us to help rebuild the land of Israel, restore the city of Jerusalem, and cause your people everywhere to draw closer to your service.

L   Then shall we, with a new song and renewed fervor, give you thanks, once again, for our physical deliverance and our spiritual freedom.

A   Blessed are you, O Lord our God, King of the universe, who created the fruit of the vine.

(Second cup of wine is drunk.)

RACHATZ

L   As we prepare to partake of the meal, we shall wash our hands, this time reciting the prescribed blessing.

A   Blessed are you, O Lord our God, King of the universe, who has sanctified us by your commandments and has commanded us concerning the washing of the hands.

(One person takes bowl and towel to all at table.)

MOTZEE MATZAH

(The remainder of the middle matzah on the plate is broken into pieces and distributed to all.)

A   Blessed are you, O Lord our God, King of the universe, who brings forth bread from the earth.

A   Blessed are you, O Lord our God, King of the universe, who has sanctified us by your commandments and has commanded us to eat matzah.

(The piece of matzah is eaten.)

MOROR

(Place both bitter herb and charoset on the top matzah cake: break it into pieces and distribute to all.)

L   We shall now partake of the moror, combined with the charoset. Thus, we remember how bitter is slavery and how it can be sweetened by God's redemption. We recite together:

A   Blessed are you, O Lord our God, King of the universe, who has sanctified us by your commandments and has commanded us to eat the bitter herbs.

(Moror and charoset are eaten.)

KORAYCH

(Leader breaks bottom matzah and distributes it to all. All assembled place some bitter herbs between two pieces of matzah and say:)

A   In ancient times, the revered sage, Hillel, observed literally the biblical commandment concerning the eating of the Pesach with matzah and moror. It is

רַחַץ

מַצָּה

מָרוֹר

כּוֹרֵךְ

stated: "With matzah and moror shall they eat it." Thus, did he combine them, even as we now do, and eat them together.

(All eat combined matzah and moror. A child or children should now hide the Afikomen for later ransom.)

שֻׁלְחָן עוֹרֵךְ

SHULCHAN ORAYCH

(The dinner is now served. At the close of the meal you may wish to sing HEVENU SHALOM.)

Hevenu Shalom

He - ve - nu sha - lom a - le-chem, he - ve - nu sha - lom a - le - chem, he - ve - nu sha - lom a - le-chem, he - ve - nu sha - lom, sha - lom, sha - lom a - le-chem

Translation
We bring greetings of peace.

צָפוּן

TZOFUN

(When the dinner is completed, the leader distributes the Afikomen, the half of the middle matzah, which had been previously set aside. If the Afikomen has been taken by one of the children, the leader must now ransom it back with money. The matzah is broken into a sufficient number of pieces to distribute to all assembled.)

L "Afikomen" means dessert. In ancient times, the Paschal lamb was the last food to be eaten. In its place we now partake of this piece of Afikomen, with which our meal is completed.

(All eat piece of matzah.)

BORAYCH

(Wine cups are filled.)

בָּרֵךְ

L Let us now recite grace.

A Let us bless God's name forever and ever.

L On behalf of all those assembled at this table we offer thanks to God for the food which we have eaten.

A Blessed be he of whose bounties we have partaken and whose goodness feeds the entire world. In mercy you provide sustenance for all living creatures. The blessing of food has never failed us, for in your goodness you do provide for all our needs.

L At this time we remember also many of your other blessings from which we and our people have benefited in the past and do benefit in the present. To our ancestors you gave a land beautiful and spacious, where they found peace and contentment after centuries of bondage. In our time, too, you blessed the untiring efforts to rebuild the land of Israel and granted your protection to our people who built it. We also remember the Holy Covenant you made with us as a people and the noble way of life you taught us through the sacred Torah which you gave us.

A Above all, we are grateful for the blessing of life and for the privilege of enjoying the beauty and goodness of the world around us. For all these, we give thanks to you and praise you. Blessed are you, O God, for the world in which we live and for the food which sustains us.

L We ask for your loving protection over our people everywhere—in this land, in Israel, and wherever they may be found. May we be spared sorrow and adversity, and may we never suffer shame or humiliation. We hope for the privilege always to be able to provide for our own needs, looking for help and support only to you.

A On this Passover, may our prayers be acceptable to you. We pray, also, that the memory of our ancestors and our people's devotion to you shall always be acceptable in your sight.

L On this festival of freedom we pray that liberty will come to all people, that a happy life of peace and contentment will be the possession of all. Bless us on this day and on every day. You who deal kindly with all creatures, we pray you to deal kindly also with us.

L May God, who is merciful, bless this home and all homes everywhere. May he bless this table upon which we have eaten, with plenty and abundance.

A Amen

L May God, who is merciful, bless those who are assembled at this table, their loved ones, their families and friends, even as he blessed our patriarchs, Abraham, Isaac, and Jacob.

A Amen

L The Lord will never forsake the righteous nor shall their children ever hunger for bread.

A May the Lord give strength unto his people; may he bless them with peace.

(The wine cups are raised.)

L Behold, we are about to partake of the third cup of wine, in gratitude for the freedom which the Lord granted our ancestors and in thankfulness for the earth's bounties of which we have eaten.

A Blessed are you, O Lord our God, King of the universe, who created the fruit of the vine.

(Drink third cup of wine.)

17

ELIJAH, THE PROPHET

L Throughout our people's history, Elijah, the prophet, has been the beloved character pictured in legends as the bearer of good tidings.

A Jewish legend recalls the mystical appearance of Elijah in times of trouble, to promise relief and redemption, to lift downcast spirits and to plant hope in the hearts of the downtrodden.

L Jewish tradition states that Elijah's greatest mission shall come when the Messiah will appear on earth, to usher in the long-promised era of permanent peace and tranquillity. For it will be Elijah, the prophet, who will precede the Messiah and will announce his arrival and, with him, the arrival of freedom and peace for all people.

A On this Seder night, when we pray for freedom, we invoke the memory of the beloved Elijah. May his spirit enter our home at this hour, and every home, bringing a message of hope for the future, faith in the goodness of people, and the assurance that freedom will come to all. We now welcome Elijah, beloved guest, at our Seder, as we rise.

(All rise. One person opens the front door of the house, leaving it open for the recitation that follows.)

A Direct your wrath, O God, upon evil and persecution. Protect your people Israel from those who would destroy them. May the spirit of Elijah, who enters our home at this hour, enter the hearts of all people. May he inspire them to love you and may he fill them with the desire to build a good world, one in which justice and freedom shall be the inheritance of all (Mal. 3:1-7).

(The leader or a selected vocalist will chant the song on the following page. All remain standing until the door is closed.)

L We await the coming of the Prophet Elijah. May he appear, bringing the Messiah with him.

(The door is closed. All are seated. The cups are filled with wine.)

L Let us now praise God, in the traditional words of the Hallel, for the many blessings which he bestows on us and for the goodness which he daily grants us:

L How shall I repay the Lord for all the good things he has done for me?

A I will lift up the cup of salvation and call upon the name of the Lord.

L I will fulfill my vows to the Lord in the presence of all his people.

A Precious in the sight of the Lord is the death of his servants.

L O Lord, I am your servant; I am your servant and the child of your handmaid; you have freed me from my bonds.

A I will offer you the sacrifice of thanksgiving and call upon the name of the Lord.

L I will fulfill my vows to the Lord in the presence of all his people.

A In the courts of the Lord's house, in the midst of you, O Jerusalem. Hallelujah!

L Praise the Lord, all you nations; laud him, all you peoples.

A For his loving-kindness toward us is great, and the faithfulness of the Lord endures forever. Hallelujah!

L Give thanks to the Lord, for he is good; his mercy endures forever.

A Let Israel now proclaim, "His mercy endures forever."

L Let the house of Aaron now proclaim, "His mercy endures forever."

A Let those who fear the Lord now proclaim, "His mercy endures forever." (Ps. 116:12–118:4).

Eliyahu Hanavi

E - li-ya - hu ha - na-vi, E - li-ya - hu ha - tish-bi,

`E - li-ya - hu, E - li-ya - hu, E - li-ya - hu ha gil - a - di.

Bim-he - ra v'ya - me - nu ya - vo a - le - nu

im - ma-shi - ach ben Da-vid, im - ma-shi - ach ben Da-vid.

E - li-ya - hu ha - na-vi, E - li-ya - hu ha - tish-bi,

E - li-ya - hu, E - li-ya - hu, E - li-ya - hu ha - na-vi,

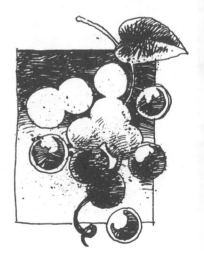

Translation
May the prophet Elijah come soon, in our time, with the Messiah, son of David.

THE EARTH'S BOUNTIES

(The cups of wine are raised.)

L We now partake of the fourth and final cup of wine as we recite together:

A Blessed are you, O Lord our God, King of the universe, who created the fruit of the vine.

(Drink the last cup of wine.)

L Blessed are you, O Lord our God, King of the universe, for the wine, fruit of the vine, and for all the bountiful produce of the field. We give thanks to you for all your goodness to us and for your loving-kindness. Blessed are you, O God, for the earth and for the fruit of the vine.

NIRTZOH

נִרְצָה

L The prescribed order of the Passover service is now complete. We have retold the ancient story of Israel's liberation. We have partaken of the traditional foods, symbols of the struggle for human freedom.

A As we have been privileged to observe the Seder tonight, may all of us be privileged to celebrate it together again next year. May it be God's will to preserve us in life and in good health.

L May the spirit of this festival remain with us throughout the coming year, and may we be imbued at all times with its lofty and exalted teachings.

A May Zion be blessed with peace and may our people and all humankind live in harmony and contentment. Amen

APPENDIX

MENU

In general, do not serve any kind of bread or use any flour products to prepare the meal. Matzah flour and meal marked specifically for Passover use is all that is allowed. Consult recipes for matzah rolls.

Passover matzah may be eaten with the meal, if desired.

Absolutely no ham or pork should be served or used. Milk also should be avoided entirely. In fact, it is recommended to avoid all dairy products with a meat dinner. Many Jewish families remain kosher by not mixing meat and milk. *(Nondairy cream may be served for the coffee.)*

Appetizer

Soups

—Chicken with matzah balls or small kosher egg noodles
—Vegetable
—Broth *(consommé)*
—Borscht *(serve hot or cold)*

Salads

—Gefilte fish *(serve hot or cold)*
—Hard-boiled eggs dipped in salt water

Entrees

(All meats and poultry must be labeled kosher.)

Chicken *(Inexpensive, generally acceptable, easy to prepare; can be fried with mix of matzah meal and seasonings. Oil used must be kosher.)*

Brisket of beef

Roast lamb

Turkey

STORY OF THE FOUR CHILDREN

WHAT DOES THE WISE CHILD SAY? *"What are the rules that God commands us to keep?"* We should tell them every rule regarding the Passover, including the rule regarding the Afikomen.

WHAT DOES THE WICKED CHILD SAY? *"What good is this service to you?"* To *you,* he means, and not to himself. And because he excludes himself from the group, it demonstrates that he does not believe in one of the most important principles. Say to him, *"I do this because the Lord helped me when I left Egypt"*—helped me, and not him. For if he had been there, he would not have been saved.

WHAT DOES THE SIMPLE CHILD SAY? *"What is all this for?"* Tell such, *"By strength of hand the Lord took us out of the land of Egypt, out of the house of slaves."*

AND FOR THE CHILD WHO IS TOO YOUNG to know how to ask, you tell him or her that the Bible says: *"On that day you should tell your children, 'I do this because the Lord helped me when I went out of Egypt.'"*

In the beginning our forefathers worshiped other gods, but the Lord who is everywhere brought us close, to worship him. The Old Testament tells us, "Joshua said to the whole people: 'This is what the Lord God of Israel has said: "Your forefathers always lived on the other side of the River. One of them was Terah, father of Abraham and Nahor. They worshiped other gods. And I took your father Abraham from the other side of the River, and I led him through all the land of Canaan. Then I gave him many children, and I gave him Isaac. And I gave Isaac, Jacob and Esau. I gave Mount Seir to Esau to own. And Jacob and his sons went down to Egypt." ' "

Blessed is he who keeps his promise to Israel because the Lord had decided in advance when he would free us, as he promised our father Abraham in a covenant. The Old Testament tells us: "The Lord said to Abram: 'Know that your children shall be enslaved and oppressed four hundred years. But I will in turn punish the nation for which they slave, and then they shall leave with great wealth.' "

It is this promise that helps our ancestors and us. Not one person alone has risen up to destroy us, because they have risen up to destroy us in every generation. But the Lord, blessed is he, saves us from their hand.

LEGENDS TOLD AT SEDER

(Optional)

The Israelite Children

This is a story that Rabbi Hanan used to tell: What do you think the Israelite women used to do? They would hide their children in caves. Then Egyptian women would bring their children to the homes of the Israelites and pinch them until they cried. The Jewish babies would hear the cries and begin crying too, and then the Egyptians would carry the Jewish children away and throw them into the Nile.

At the same time the Lord said to his angels: "Go down from heaven and look at how the children of my favorites, Abraham, Isaac, and Jacob, are being thrown into the Nile."

The angels rushed down and stood in water up to their knees, taking the Jewish babies and laying them on the rocks; and God made milk and honey flow from the rocks so the children could suckle.

Then a great miracle happened—the babies were swallowed up in the ground not far from the Nile. The Egyptians brought oxen to dig up the ground over them. But after the Egyptians left, the children began sprouting from the earth like grass. And when they were finished growing, they walked back home. Later, when God showed himself over the Red Sea, these children were the first to recognize him, and they sang songs of praise to him.

Young Moses

When Pharaoh's daughter brought Moses back with her to the palace she would hug and kiss him as though he were her very own, and she let him live. Moses was a rather handsome child and everyone enjoyed being in his presence.

Pharaoh, too, would kiss and hug him, and Moses would remove the crown off Pharaoh's head and place it on his own. The Egyptian priests were present and warned Pharaoh that this was a sign that Moses would take his kingdom away from him.

Some of the priests wanted Moses killed, but there was a wise man among them who suggested that Pharaoh test the child. So they placed a plate with gold and a hot coal in front of him. If he picked up the gold it would mean that he understood what he was doing and he should be killed. But if he picked up the hot coal it would mean that he had no sense and should not die.

The plate was brought to Moses. He began to reach toward the gold, but Gabriel, the angel, pushed his hand to the hot coal. Moses picked it up and placed it in his mouth. His tongue was burned, and for that reason Moses always had difficulty talking and relied on his brother, Aaron, to help him.

GLOSSARY

Afikomen (ah-fée-ko-men) dessert matzah; one-half of the middle matzah

B'chol (b'kúl) personal deliverance
Boraych (bow-róck) grace after meal
Brachah (bráh-kah) blessing

Chametz (káh-mets) leaven
Charoset (káre-o-set) mixture of chopped apples, walnuts, cinnamon, and grape wine

Dayenu (díe-ah-new) enough

Eliyahu Hanavi (e-lee-yáh-who hah-náh-vee) Elijah the Prophet

Haggadah (háh-gah-dah) the Jewish ritual for the Seder
Hallel (hah-láil) psalms; literally, praise
Hevenu Shalom Alechem (hay-veh-néw shah-loám ah-lećk-em) ''We bring greetings of peace''

Kadaysh (káy-dash) to sanctify
Karpas (kár-pas) green vegetable
Koraych (ko-ráhch) bitter herbs and matzah combined

Mageed (ma-geéd) recite
Matzah (máh-tzah) unleavened bread
Matzot (máh-tzot) unleavened bread, plural
Mitzvah (mĭts-vah) joy
Moror (mów-roar) bitter herb
Motzee (moat-sáy) breaking and eating remainder of middle matzah on the plate (not afikomen piece)

Nirtzoh (neár-tzoh) closing prayer; literally, the acceptance

Pesach (páy-sak) the Passover

Rachatz (ráh-hots) washing hands, with blessing

Seder (sáy-der) Passover meal and ritual
Shulchan Oraych (shúle-kahn ó-rock) the dinner served

Torah (tóe-rah) wisdom and law in Jewish Scripture; the Pentateuch, first five books of Moses
Tzafun (tza-fún) distribution of dessert

Urchatz (úr-kots) washing of hands, without blessing

Yachatz (yáh-hots) breaking the matzah; literally, to divide